Fast Food Felicity

Written by Jenny Hargreave

Illustrated by Trish Hill

Contents

Page

Rigby

Fast Food Felicity

With these characters ...

Felicity
O'Fingle

Felicity's
Mechanic

"I'm Fast Food Felicity,

Felicity O'Fingle loves fast food.
Every day she drives her old red car
into town to buy her favorite fast foods.

    One day, Felicity's car breaks down.
Then she learns that it is important
to put the right things into cars — *and*
into your body. Felicity also learns
that fast foods are not *always* the right
things!

I love to eat my fries ...″

Felicity O'Fingle loved to eat fast food. She loved hamburgers and cheeseburgers. She loved cupcakes and donuts. She loved hot dogs, french fries, and pizzas. She loved milk shakes and fizzy drinks.

She loved those foods and drinks so much, that her friends called her "Fast Food Felicity."

Fast Food Felicity always drove her old red car to fast food places. She thought that walking or riding a bike was too healthy.

While she drove, Felicity made up songs.

One day, on her way to the burger stand, Felicity made up a new song.

"I'm Fast Food Felicity,
I love to eat my fries.
The only foods
I like to eat more,
are burgers,
cupcakes, and pies!"

She drove past the fruit and vegetable stand, past the supermarket, and past the bakery. When Felicity arrived at the burger stand, she could smell her favorite foods.

Felicity stopped her old car by the menu. She wound down the window and licked her lips.

Then she ordered a hamburger, fries, and a milk shake. Felicity reminded them *not* to put any vegetables on her hamburger.

Felicity was so hungry, she gulped down her food and guzzled her milk shake in the parking lot.

On her way home, she sang a new verse for her song.

"With a lick of my lips,
and a wiggle of my hips,
I drive each day to town.
When I get there,
I stop and stare,
and choose what I'll now gulp down!"

When she arrived home, her car jerked
up the driveway and creaked to a stop.
Felicity saw steam coming out from
under her car's hood. She also heard
a gurgling sound. It sounded like
someone blowing bubbles in a milk shake.
Then she smelled something strange.

"Oh, no! Something stinks," sniffed
Felicity. "I'm going inside!"

Felicity went inside and took off
her shoes. She sat cross-legged
on her favorite chair. Felicity tried
to concentrate on the TV. But all
she could think about was dinner.

"I feel like pizza, ice cream, and soda
tonight!" said Fast Food Felicity.

That night, Felicity's car jerked and creaked all the way back to town. She didn't worry about the steam coming out from under the hood. So she sang a new verse for her song.

"Cakes and pies, burgers and fries. Oh, how I love them so. Pizza and cheese! More ice cream, please! Then homeward I will go."

Chapter 2

With her delicious
ham and cheese
pizza, Felicity
started to drive
home. She wound
up the windows
so that its delicious
smell would not
escape. She
sniffed happily.

Suddenly, Felicity's car wasn't jerking and creaking. It was croaking to a stop! Even more steam was coming out from under the car's hood.

"Oh, no," said Felicity. She looked at the dashboard. A red light flashed. The needle in the temperature gauge pointed to red, for hot.

While Felicity was thinking about what to do, she ate her pizza.

Temperature

"I mustn't let my pizza get cold," she grinned. Then she had a great idea.

"Cold! Of course! I'll put something cold into my engine. My ice cream and soda will cool down its temperature."

She hated the idea of wasting her ice cream and soda. But she hated the idea of walking home even more.

She lifted the hood and carefully poured the soda into the engine. Then she dropped in two scoops of ice cream.

"That will cool it down," she said. And it did. But for how long?

Felicity's car jerked and crunched down the road. Then, it stopped again!

"What now?" thought Felicity. She frowned at the dashboard. Another red light flashed. This time, the needle in the oil gauge pointed to "E" for empty.

Felicity walked along the street to a supermarket. She needed oil quickly.

Felicity looked at all the cooking oils. There were bottles of olive oil, canola oil, peanut oil, and sunflower oil. Felicity chose a bottle with the label "Deep Fry" on it. She knew that she could use the leftover oil to fry frozen french fries.

Back at her car, Felicity poured most of the "Deep Fry" oil into the engine. Her car jerked and crunched back home.

A cloud of black smoke poured out from the back of her car. A cloud of steam poured out from the front of her car.

With a loud bang, the car stopped in her driveway. Felicity wondered what she had done wrong. Maybe she should have used olive oil. Or were two scoops of ice cream too much?

Chapter 3.

The next day, Felicity's car was towed to the garage. Her mechanic loved cars almost as much as Felicity loved fast food.

"You poured soda and cooking oil into the engine!" she said in disgust. "And you added ice cream!" she said in disbelief. The mechanic shook her head from side to side.

"You can't put those things in a car's engine!" said the mechanic. "A car is like a person. Just like we need healthy food, a car needs the right things to run properly, too. You wouldn't eat unhealthy food *every* day, would you?"

Felicity's face turned the same color as her car!

Felicity didn't know what to say,
so she shrugged her shoulders.
She looked guilty.

"If we put the wrong things into the
engine, it won't last long at all. So let's
put the right things into your engine,
and your car will last a lifetime,"
said the mechanic.

"Oh, really? A lifetime?" said Felicity.

After Felicity left the mechanic's, she felt upset. She thought about the unhealthy food she ate *every* day. How long might she last?

"Poor me. But I love fast food," Felicity thought. She decided to try and eat healthy foods. Just then, her tummy rumbled. What would she decide to eat?

Chapter 4.

Felicity panted and puffed all the way into town. She saw the hamburger stand ahead.

Felicity *really* wanted to stop there for a hamburger and french fries. But her panting and puffing reminded her of her car's engine blowing out steam. "I *must* eat healthy food," she said over and over again.

Felicity saw more fast food places.
Their bright lights flashed on and off.
Luckily, the lights reminded her of
the red flashing lights in her car.
She walked quickly past every one of
them.

Felicity's legs were tired. She couldn't walk any further. Her tummy felt sore. Felicity needed food — NOW! Suddenly, she saw two words on a store window — "FAST FOOD!"

Felicity staggered inside the store. She felt like she might faint.

"Quick, give . . . me . . . some . . . fast food!" she panted. Then she looked around. She was in shock. What was this? This was *not* fast food. She was in a fruit and vegetable store!

She looked at the window again.
This time, she saw another two words
above "FAST FOOD!"

"Try Nature's . . ." she read slowly.
"Try Nature's FAST FOOD!"

The storekeeper smiled and handed
a banana to Felicity.

"A banana has a natural wrapping, is easy to take with you, and it's ready to eat now!" the storekeeper said. "It's one of the best fast foods!"

Felicity peeled the banana and took a bite.

"Mmmm," said Felicity. "Natural fast food!" Now THAT was an idea that she liked! "What other fast food do you sell?" she asked.

"Have a look around," said the storekeeper. And Felicity did.

"This is great," she thought. "I can eat as much of this fast food as I want. Now I can tell my mechanic I *am* putting the right things into my body!"

And, as she walked happily home, Felicity sang a new song.

"No more burgers, no more cupcakes, no pizza, nothing fried!
Nothing but the best, forget the rest, only good food goes inside!"

"I'm Fast Food Felicity, only healthy food for me!
The only fast food I will eat is fast food from a tree!"

"Fresh, delicious"

Fruit

Fresh, delicious

Nature's fast food

Ready to take home

Healthy!